Our Man

A Play

Daniel Clucas

Samuel French – London
New York – Sydney – Toronto – Hollywood

Copyright © 1984 by Daniel Clucas
All Rights Reserved

OUR MAN is fully protected under the copyright laws of the British Commonwealth, including Canada, the United States of America, and all other countries of the Copyright Union. All rights, including professional and amateur stage productions, recitation, lecturing, public reading, motion picture, radio broadcasting, television and the rights of translation into foreign languages are strictly reserved.

ISBN 978-0-573-12187-6

www.samuelfrench.co.uk
www.samuelfrench.com

FOR AMATEUR PRODUCTION ENQUIRIES

UNITED KINGDOM AND WORLD EXCLUDING NORTH AMERICA
plays@SamuelFrench-London.co.uk
020 7255 4302/01

Each title is subject to availability from Samuel French, depending upon country of performance.

CAUTION: Professional and amateur producers are hereby warned that OUR MAN is subject to a licensing fee. Publication of this play does not imply availability for performance. Both amateurs and professionals considering a production are strongly advised to apply to the appropriate agent before starting rehearsals, advertising, or booking a theatre. A licensing fee must be paid whether the title is presented for charity or gain and whether or not admission is charged.

The professional rights in this play are controlled by Samuel French Ltd, 52 Fitzroy Street, London, W1T 5JR.

No one shall make any changes in this title for the purpose of production. No part of this book may be reproduced, stored in a retrieval system, or transmitted in any form, by any means, now known or yet to be invented, including mechanical, electronic, photocopying, recording, videotaping, or otherwise, without the prior written permission of the publisher. No one shall upload this title, or part of this title, to any social media websites.

The right of Daniel Clucas be identified as author of this work has been asserted in accordance with Section 77 of the Copyright, Designs and Patents Act 1988.

OUR MAN

First produced by Andrew Fell for the Stage Craft Theatre Company at the Lyric Studio, Hammersmith on the 30th March 1983, with the following list of characters:

Phones	Andre Winterton
Sir	Maurice Thorogood
Eyes	Pip Short
Ears	Daniel Clucas
Nose	Derek Chapman
Mouth	Simon Haywood

Directed by Andrew Fell
Designed by Eugenie Hedley

The action takes place inside the head of Private Jones

OUR MAN*

It is the inside of Private Jones's head

When the CURTAIN *rises the stage is dark except for the blue light of a TV screen. There is a food tube for Mouth, and a screen with shutters for Eyes. Files and a progress report lie on Phones' desk, together with a microphone. Phones sits at the desk wearing earphones. Unless he is addressing someone on stage, Phones speaks into the microphone*

Phones Sir.

Sir (*off*) What is it, Phones?

Phones I'm getting a reading from the rib cage. I think we're being kicked.

Sir (*off*) Why should anyone want to kick us?

Phones Our Man's asleep.

Sir (*off*) That's why we're being kicked. Someone's trying to wake us up. I'll be right there, Phones.

After a pause Sir enters

Where are we, Phones?

Phones I'm not too sure, Sir. If you wake Our Man up I'll be able to say.

Sir Where's Eyes?

Phones (*pointing to the TV screen*) There, Sir.

Sir What's he doing?

Phones He's participating in the dream, Sir.

Sir (*into the microphone*) Get up here, will you, Eyes? (*To Phones*) Where's the rest?

Phones (*flicking the TV channel*) That's Ears.

Sir Uh-huh.

Phones (*flicking the channel*) That's Nose.

---

*N.B. Paragraph 3 on page ii of this Acting Edition regarding photocopying and video-recording should be carefully read.

Sir That's part of the dream as well, is it?
Phones Yes, Sir. (*He flicks the channel again*) And that's Mouth.
Sir Good grief. Call them all back, Phones.
Phones Sir.

Eyes enters

Sir Ah, Eyes. Get to your post will you and open up.
Eyes Sir. (*He goes and sits in front of the screen with shutters*)
Phones (*flicking the channel*) Come back, Ears.

Light seeps in as Eyes opens the shutters

Sir Let's see where we are.
Phones (*flicking the channel*) Come back, Nose. Mouth, come back.
Eyes It looks like daylight.
Sir Can you tell who's kicking us?
Eyes Not at this angle. Shall I open up further?
Sir No. That's far enough for now. Ears! Where's Ears?

Ears enters, changing out of his dream costume

Ears Here, Sir.
Sir Ah, good. What .... ? Get to your post. See if someone's talking to us. Are Nose and Mouth on their way?
Phones Should be here any moment, Sir.
Sir Good.
Ears I can just make it out, Sir.
Sir Yes? What's he saying?
Ears "Wake up, Jones."
Sir Jones. That's us. Where are we, Phones?
Phones Base camp. We enter enemy territory today, Sir. I think Our Man's programmed to wake at six a.m.

Nose and Mouth enter

Sir What's Our Man's first objective for the day?
Phones Get up and have breakfast.
Nose Pwah! What a stench!
Sir All right, let's get things in order. Eyes, open wide, get ready for the light. Ears, clean your lugholes out. Back to your post, Nose.
Nose Pwah, sir, it smells awful!

Our Man

Mouth It's not surprising, the whole platoon under the same roof.
Sir You ready, Mouth?
Mouth Sir. (*He prepares himself*)
Sir Come on. Lord knows what you were doing in that dream half way up Nelson's column sucking a coconut.
Eyes I can see a large black boot with a leg sticking out of it and as I look higher I can see the sarge looking down at us, a bush of black hairs sticking from his nose.
Mouth Right, ready.
Sir Morning, Sarge.
Mouth Morning, Sarge.
Sir Any reply, Ears?
Ears "Get up, Jones."
Mouth Shall I reply?
Sir I don't think that's necessary, Mouth. What do you see, Eyes?
Eyes Brown, dusty air. Dirty floor boards. Canteen table. Platoon grouped around it. Bedding wrapped up against the wall.
Sir What?
Eyes I think we're the last man up.
Sir Out of the whole platoon?
Eyes Yes, Sir.
Sir Right.
Ears I can hear the sharp tinkle of canteen cutlery, scraping of plates, and——
Sir Yes, all right, thank you, Ears. That'll do. That'll do. Come on, snap out of it. Let's get Our Man moving. We're a machine, not a body. A lethal fighting machine. What are we?
All (*unenthusiastically*) A lethal fighting machine.
Sir Up. Up. Get him out of bed.
Phones Get out of bed.
Sir Get up.
Phones Get up.
Sir Stretch Legs. Arms. Shoulders. Back. Stretch everything.
Phones Legs stretch.
Mouth (*in sympathy with the stretching*) Awwww!
Sir That's right. Stretch the Legs.
Phones Arms and Shoulders stretch.
Mouth Mmm!
Sir What do you hear, Ears?
Phones Back stretch.

Mouth (*groaning loudly*) Aw!
Ears Nothing with him groaning away.
Sir Don't overdo it, Mouth.
Phones All departments stretch.
Mouth Gwah!
Sir Must you be so loud?
Mouth I do when I'm on line to CNS, I have no choice.
Sir You're attracting unnecessary attention. Can't you do it more quietly?
Mouth I'll do my best.
Sir What do you see, Eyes?
Phones Every department, one last time, right through, Toes to the Head.
Eyes Cobwebs, dust and beams.
Mouth (*loudly*) Gwah!
Ears At least you can see. I can't hear a thing, thanks to him.
Phones Body reports atmosphere outside as chilly.
Mouth Fwah! I'm freezing!
Phones The Toes especially claim to be very cold.
Mouth Fwah! Me toes! Me flaming toes!
Eyes (*to Ears*) Can you imagine what this place must have been like in the old days?
Ears Yeah.
Sir Put the socks on them, Phones.
Ears Organ music.
Eyes We've already got socks on.
Nose They need changing.
Eyes Women in their Sunday best.
Sir Then put the boots on.
Ears Church choirs singing.
Mouth You're taxing Our Man a bit aren't you, this early in the morning?

Ears starts to sing and hum "Bringing in the Sheaves" in the background

Sir Give the order, Phones.
Phones Put on the boots.
Eyes Men in their best suits.
Phones (*into the microphone; to the hands and arms*) Well, I don't know do I?

Eyes They're on our right.
Phones They're on our right.
Eyes That's the left. We want the right.
Phones You're going the wrong way. You want to go to the right. Which Hand do we write with?
Eyes Left Hand is signalling.
Phones You're signalling the left Hand. We write with the right Hand.
Sir It is early in the morning, isn't it.
Eyes They've found the boots.
Sir Bring the Foot up to the Hands, Phones.
Phones Which one?
Sir I don't know. Any one. Does it matter?
Phones If we bring them both up at the same time we fall over.
Sir Yes, all right. Bring up the right one.
Phones Right Foot up towards boot.

Ears, to the same tune, sings "Putting on the boot, putting on the boot. Early in the morning, putting on the boot."

Sir Insert.
Phones Insert right Foot into boot.
Mouth Ouch!
Phones Try again.
Eyes It's there.
Ears Oi, Mouth. Come on.

Ears gives Mouth the tune and they both start to sing in the background, "Putting on the Boot". Mouth is out of tune

Phones Congratulations, Hands, you made it.

The singing gets louder

(*Trying to speak over the noise*) Is it ... Is it too much to ask ... Is it too much to ask ...?
Sir Shut up, Mouth.

Mouth stops singing

Phones Is it too much to ask for you to tie up the laces?
Ears You're way out of tune, Mouth.
Eyes (*to Nose*) What is a minister doing when he rehearses a sermon?

Phones He can go for days singing the same song and never hit a right note. It's a gift.

Eyes Practising what he preaches.

Phones You'll find the laces at the top of the boot, near where the Leg sticks out. Where else would they be?

Ears Mouth. (*Ears quietly demonstrates to Mouth in the background how the song should go*)

Eyes Hang about. One of them's tucked inside the boot.

Phones Hold on. Apparently, one of the laces is caught up inside the boot. Is Forefinger there?

Eyes It's the left Forefinger we need.

Phones Left Forefinger?

Nose No. He's busy.

Phones Can't that wait?

Nose If I'm to fulfil my function, I need to have clean tubes.

Sir Cancel your demand, Nose. We need left Forefinger down there.

Nose All right. But if I don't perform my job properly, don't blame me. You can go now, left Forefinger. Thank you very much.

During the following Ears and Mouth start to sing to the same tune "Picking at the nose, picking at the nose, picking at the bogeys, picking at the nose"

Eyes (*to Nose*) What do you get if you cross a centipede with a turkey?

Nose Shut up.

Eyes A Thanksgiving. Everyone would get a leg.

Phones Left Forefinger? I want—I want ... Are you there, left Forefinger?

Sir Shut up. Everyone shut up!

They do

Phones Left Forefinger. I want you to hook yourself under the lace caught up on the left hand side of the right Foot and retrieve it from the boot ... You've got a bit of what? No. Flick it away. Don't wipe it on the sock.

Eyes He's done it.

Phones Right. Now, pull out that lace.

Eyes The lace is out.

Phones Thank you, left Forefinger.
Sir Carry on, Phones. (*He moves away to study a progress report*)
Phones Right. We're going to tie the lace now. You ready, Hands? Right Hand take right lace. Left Hand take left lace. This is the right Foot we're talking about now. You got that? Pull them together.
Eyes It's there.
Phones Cross them over. Well, which way do you usually do it? I don't know. You should know.
Eyes We're being watched.
Sir Ignore them.
Phones Try right over left.
Eyes Wrong.
Phones Left over right.
Eyes That's it.
Phones Swap Hands.
Ears They're talking about us.
Sir Take no notice.
Eyes They've dropped the laces.
Phones When I said swap Hands, you're supposed to swap laces too. Not drop them. We've done it enough times before.
Eyes They've picked them up.
Ears "Lazy bugger, Jones."
Phones Let's try it again. Right Hand take left lace from left Hand. Left Hand take right lace from right Hand.
Ears "What's the matter? Can't you tie your own boot lace?"
Eyes It's there. That was Flemings.
Mouth Sod off, Flemings.
Phones Left lace over right lace, then under right lace.
Eyes It's there.
Phones Good. Pull tight. Left Thumb out. Right Hand, loop right hanging lace over left Thumb, joining the right hanging lace's two lengths together by the knot . . .
Eyes It's there.
Ears "A monkey could do better."
Eyes That was Parsons.
Sir Ignore it.
Phones Take out left Thumb.
Nose I can smell bacon and eggs. I think. Maybe canteen coffee.

Everyone groans

Phones Left Hand ... *Left* Hand. You got that? Left Hand pull left hanging lace round right Hand's loop, leaving it on the right Hand's Thumb. Right Hand Thumb and right Hand Forefinger pinch it and lead it ... Keep hold of it though. Lead it through right Hand Thumb's loop.
Eyes Yes, it's coffee they're drinking. I can see it now. And I think ...
Phones Left Hand Forefinger and Thumb collect the left hanging lace peeping through right Hand Thumb's loop ...
Eyes It's bacon and eggs with beans.

Everyone groans.

Phones The stomach can't take any more beans, Sir. (*Into the microphone*) Right, now pull it through.
Sir Go easy on the beans, Mouth.
Phones Pull it through. You got that?
Ears Someone's just called us a lazy wally.
Sir Who was that? Hesketh?
Eyes Yes, it was Hesketh all right.
Phones At the same time ...
Sir Tell him he's a twit, Mouth.
Mouth Shut your face, doss-head!
Sir Mmm.
Mouth You've got to put him in his place, Sir. You know Hesketh.
Phones At the same time right Hand Forefinger and Thumb take right hanging loop and pull that away from the knot. This should give us a bow. You got that? (*He pauses*) The little bunny rabbit runs round the tree, peeps through the hole, has his nose pinched and his tail pulled ...
Eyes It's there. It's there.
Phones Could you manage the other shoe by yourselves? The left boot, in case you're wondering, goes on to the left Foot. That's the Foot next to the right Foot, which has a boot on already. It shouldn't be too difficult.
Eyes (*to Nose*) What did the boot say to the foot?
Sir Phones. Delve into the Memory file will you. How did that last bit of conversation we had with Hesketh go last night?
Eyes Eh? What did the boot say?
Mouth Ouch!

Our Man

Eyes Hands have just caught left Little Toe on boot.
Phones Left Hand slap right Hand. Right Hand slap left Hand. (*To Sir*) Where would you like it to go from, Sir? (*He leafs through a file*)
Sir Towards the end of the conversation.
Eyes The boot said to the foot, "You're putting me on."

Nose ignores him

Phones (*reading*) "It's between you and Flemings."
Sir That'll do.
Phones Minutes from yesterday's conversation with Hesketh, ten twenty-five p.m. Hesketh says "It's between you and Flemings, I would say. You've both served as long——"
Eyes We were sitting on two old oil drums, front of the church. Hesketh here. Our Man there. Sitting under an umbrella of dark crimson sky, speckled with deep mauve strata clouds ...
Ear Ducks wings beating low over us. Making for the south ...
Eyes That's right, and——
Ears And in the distance, gunfire. Pounding ...
Sir Shut up.
Phones "I know Flemings wants it, did you see the way he took charge out on the field today?" Our Man replied—(*He turns the page*) Our Man ... Our Man didn't reply. Hesketh continued "I tell you, Jones, keep your nose clean and don't let him get one over you."
Sir And here we are last up out of the whole platoon.
Eyes The boots have been laced up.
Sir Let's have breakfast.
Phones Right Leg. Bedding against the wall. All appropriate departments walk to canteen table for coffee, breakfast, all the usual things.
Sir Where's Flemings, Eyes?
Eyes Over on our right. He's finished breakfast and talking to Vickers.
Ears Wilkins says, "Morning, Jones".
Sir Say it back.
Mouth Morning, Wilkins.
Eyes Look out. Here comes canteen coffee.

Mouth connects the food tube

Sir Shut off, Nose. Look away, Eyes. Phones?
Phones I've notified all appropriate departments with advance warning. It should be all right. It's the beans that worry me. The stomach really doesn't seem too confident about the outcome.
Sir They'll just have to put up with it, I'm afraid.
Mouth It's coming in.
Sir Get it down fast. The quicker it's in the quicker it's out.
Eyes Eugh! That's disgusting!
Sir What is it?
Eyes It's Parsons, Sir! I've never seen him eat before! He's drooling tomato sauce all down his chin!
Ears That's nothing. You should hear him. Like a pig in a trough.
Nose He doesn't smell too good either.
Mouth Shall I tell him?

Everyone says "Yeah, go on"

Sir Leave it, Mouth. Phones?
Phones All in working order, Sir.
Sir All right. Everyone get on with their own departments but keep it clean. You hear, Mouth?
Mouth Yes, Sir.

Phones and Sir discuss the day ahead as the senses work in the background

Sir Right, Phones.
Mouth You're a pig, Parsons.
Phones Well, Sir, I figure after breakfast, having been briefed we'll be on manoeuvres as soon as possible. Probably well before seven a.m. It's certainly going to be an early start.
Sir Legs feeling sturdy?
Phones As well as might be expected, Sir.
Sir That's not good enough.
Mouth Here comes the beans.

Everyone groans

Sir They've got to be at their best.
Ears I can hear the Stomach groan from here.
Phones When things hot up they'll carry us through I'm sure.
Sir What sort of opposition can we expect today?
Phones From Flemings or the enemy?

Our Man

Sir The enemy.
Phones Hopefully not too much.
Mouth How much more is there, Eyes?
Eyes Half a plateful.

There are more varied groans

Ears You know what they say——
Mouth The quicker they're in——
All —the quicker they're out.
Phones The enemy are making a final stand in a village just to the north of here. They've been constantly harassed by fighters and heavy artillery, so by the time we get there they should be well softened up.
Sir Don't be too sure.
Phones I won't, Sir.
Ears "Why did you call me a doss-head just now, Jones?"
Eyes He's eating bacon, if that's any use.
Mouth Shut up, Hesketh, or you'll choke on your bacon rind.
Ears "You want some of my beans?"
Eyes They're disgusting. Cold and soggy.
Mouth No thanks.
Phones Don't accept those beans!
Mouth (*turning to Phones*) I know.
Ears "What's the matter? Don't you like beans?"
Mouth Not breakfast, lunch and supper seven days a week I don't.
Nose I'm smelling something funny.
Mouth What?
Nose Second-hand beans I think.
Mouth All right you lot. Own up. Who's done it?
Ears "Not me." Williams said that.
Eyes Williams said that.
Nose It was Williams.
Mouth Williams, you're a pig.
Sir Go easy on him, Mouth.
Mouth You're a very naughty boy.
Sir It could have been us.
Mouth You've dropped one, haven't you?
Nose It's a big one.
Mouth And it's a big one.

Ears Poor old Williams. Everyone else is giving him stick too now.
Phones Sir. We're getting urgent signals from the Bowels Department.
Nose I think it's one of ours.
Phones They say it's one of ours.
Mouth It's ours?
Nose I thought it was.
Sir Don't say anything else, Mouth. (*To Eyes*) Has anyone noticed?
Eyes I don't think so.
Ears They're still accusing Williams.
Sir Let's keep it that way. Just carry on with breakfast quietly and no-one will be any the wiser. What's the overall report, Phones?
Phones Everything's in fit working order, Sir.
Sir The Arms?
Phones Strong, Sir.
Sir Feet?
Phones Toes complain of blisters. Nothing serious.
Sir Neck stiff?
Eyes Phones. This last piece of bacon's all gristle.
Phones What do you want me to do about it?
Eyes Have the Hands push it to one side. You can't shove that down Stomach.
Sir Eat it. The Stomach can take care of itself.
Phones Everything's in fine shape, Sir.
Sir Good. I want this body efficient, and strong. We've got to be to beat the enemy. Quick reflexes with split-second timing. That's what's needed.
Ears What's happening out there, Eyes?
Phones I'm sure after a few shots of adrenalin you'd be lucky to find a man as fast as Our Man in the whole platoon.
Eyes They're getting ready for briefing, I think.
Sir Its distractions, Phones. I don't want any distractions. Our Man's progress chart shows we've been far too vague recently. Forget about home. Forget about everything. We're here to fight a war. The quicker we realize that, the better.
Eyes Breakfast's put away.
Sir For the time being I want Our Man working like clockwork. Efficient to the split second. Lethal. You hear?

Phones Sir.
Mouth Oi. Breakfast's put away.
Phones It's shaving next.
Sir I want Our Man shaved next, Phones.
Phones Sir.
Ears We can't shave. Barker's going to brief the platoon. Everyone down his end.
Eyes That's the altar end.
Sir Don't we have time to shave?
Eyes No.
Sir That's a pity. Better get down there then, Phones.
Eyes Down the aisle on the right, there's a spare pew.
Ears You've got to hurry though.
Phones Make for spare pew down aisle on right.
Eyes We'll be sitting next to Williams, having Flemings behind us.
Mouth We don't want to sit near Flemings.
Nose You don't have to talk to him.
Phones How we doing?
Eyes Nearly there. We're there.
Sir Sit.
Phones Sit.
Eyes We're sat.
Ears Barker's telling us to sit down.
Mouth We have sat down. Stupid prat. Oops.

There is a pause

Sir Did Barker hear that?
Eyes I don't think so.
Sir Don't you dare let that happen again, Mouth. We might have found ourself down on report.
Eyes What's this, Ears?
Ears What?
Eyes What's Barker saying to Wilkinson?
Sir You've spoken out of turn far too often recently. Don't let it happen again.
Eyes I think——
Sir The last thing we want is to be put down on report.
Ears I think he's telling Wilkinson to put Jones down on report.
Nose But Jones is us!
Eyes We're on report!

Sir Right. Put Mouth down on report, Phones.
Ears You stupid idiot, Mouth.
Nose We're on report.
Sir (*to Mouth*) I don't want to hear another word from you.
Nose We'll never get promotion now.
Eyes You're an idiot, Mouth.
Sir Listen. We still have a chance.
Phones We did well yesterday. They must take that into account.
Sir Exactly. We must do well today also. I want everyone to pay precise attention to the briefing. Every word must be absorbed. No mistakes made. We have to do well today.
Nose (*to Mouth*) Stupid prat!
Sir Ears, listen intently. Eyes, watch earnestly. There's not much you can do, Nose ... But Mouth, not another word. Understand?
Mouth Sir.
Sir What's happening, Eyes?
Eyes We're about five rows back from Barker who stands this end of the altar before a large map of the local terrain. That's including this church and enemy territory. He's speaking now.
Ears "Settle down chaps."
Sir All right. Maximum efficiency. Every word must be absorbed.
Ears "I know these briefings tend to drag, but bear with us."
Sir What was that?
Ears Um. He said—"I know these briefings tend to drag but bear with us."
Sir Then what did he say?
Ears I just missed it.
Sir Well, what's he saying now?
Ears He says we're very close to enemy territory.
Mouth We know that already.
Sir Shut up.
Mouth But all I——
Sir Shut up.
Ears Barker just said he hopes we're all feeling fit.
Sir Yes, we are.
Ears Missed that bit.
Sir What was it?
Ears Um. I don't know. Something about—oh, I can't remember. Shall I think back?

Our Man

Sir Don't bother.
Ears Something about having slept all right.
Sir Is that all?
Ears I think so.
Sir What's he saying now?
Ears Um. "Yesterday. Yesterday was a good day."
Sir Frightening day too.
Ears "Lots of good things done. Good work by Saunder's team."
Nose That's our team.
Ears "Kept your heads."
Phones Only just.
Ears "Very impressive."
Phones The amount of trouble I had keeping CNS quiet ...
Sir Ssh!
Ears "Let's hope today's as successful."
Phones My guess is another day like that and CNS would crack up.
Ears "It should be."
Sir Was it really bad?
Phones Put it this way. There were moments.
Sir How bad those moments?
Phones If we'd slowed down at all. If we'd stopped to think, we'd have lost control and ...
Sir That's the point though, isn't it? We mustn't stop to think.
Eyes Instead we rush in blind.
Sir It gets results.
Eyes Could get us killed.
Sir Anyway, from what I gather, today's going to be nothing like yesterday. Just a mopping-up operation. Is that not so?
Phones That's what we hope.
Ears He's still talking, do you want to listen?
Sir What's he said?
Ears He was telling us about enemy morale. His guess is that it must be low. They haven't had a moment's peace, er ... Then he went on to say how well he hopes we've all slept again and how lucky we are because ... because the enemy hasn't slept at all. They've been constantly bombarded by heavy artillery and air power, whatever. Their morale is low. We must capitalize on this ... That's as far as I got.
Sir And what's he saying now?

Ears Um. "They are confined ... will remain confined in this village here."
Mouth We know that already.
Sir (*to Mouth*) Did you say something?
Ears "Same as before. Splitting into three teams."
Sir (*to Mouth*) Don't you think you've done enough damage?
Ears "Brown take one."
Sir Don't you?
Mouth Sir.
Ears "Saunders the other."
Sir Then keep shut.
Ears "Mitchell, the third."
Sir Sorry, Ears, missed that. What was it he said?
Ears Splitting into three teams. Brown takes one. Saunders the other and Mitchell the third. Same as before.
Sir Then what did he say?
Ears I've missed a lot of it. Um ... Well, he's saying now ... What he's saying is ... "three pronged attack".
Sir (*to Mouth*) See.
Ears "Brown's team will take the A road."
Sir We've missed some more because of you.
Ears "To the left here."
Sir Every time you open you cause trouble.
Ears Are you listening?
Sir Yes, I'm listening.
Ears "Disembark at this farmhouse here."
Sir Just try and keep shut.
Ears You're not listening.
Sir I am listening.
Ears "Yet out of sight of the village itself."
Sir What's he said so far?
Ears I just told you.
Sir I missed it.
Ears It was about Brown's team.
Sir Not Saunders' team?
Ears No. Brown's team. He's talking about Saunders' team now.
Sir What did he say about Brown's team?
Ears Something about approaching the village from the north. Hadn't you better listen to what he has to say about our team though? Saunders' team?

Our Man

Sir Yes, you're right. What's he saying?
Ears He says ... I've missed it.
Sir You've what?
Ears Don't blame me. I was talking to you. It's your fault.
Sir It's not my fault. It's his fault.
Mouth My fault!
Sir Shut up.
Phones We've got to know our orders.
Eyes Williams is next to us. Ask him what they were.
Sir Ask him.
Mouth Different tune now you——
Sir Do as you're told!
Mouth 'Ere, Williams ...
Sir Quietly!
Mouth What was that he said about Saunders' team?
Sir Listen to this, Ears.
Ears Give us a chance (*He pauses*) Saunders' team——
Sir It's very important.
Ears "Saunders' team is to go in from here. The church. Heading directly north. The first miles will be quiet. Then you're to disembark, covering the rest of the ground on foot. At those crossroads there, on the map."
Sir Can you see it, Eyes?
Eyes Yes, I can see it.
Sir Where is it?
Eyes Shall I tell you when you've finished listening?
Sir Good idea.
Ears He wants a steady sweep north, knocking out isolated enemy positions, stragglers, as you go along.
Sir That's all we need to know.
Ears That's all there is to know.
Sir Say, thank you.
Mouth Thanks.
Sir What's being said by Barker now?
Ears Something about heading west in similar manner.
Phones He'll be talking about Mitchell's team won't he?
Sir It doesn't concern us then.
Eyes It concerns Williams, he's in Mitchell's team. He's missed it.
Sir (*to Mouth*) That's your fault again.
Mouth Me?

Sir You keep speaking out of turn. Distracting us ...
Ears Briefing hasn't finished yet. Do you want to hear it?
Sir Yes, of course I do.
Ears Barker says by lunch time the three teams should have converged on the village. Entering the centre will be hardest. When we get there he wants each team to remain spread out.
Sir This is at the village?
Ears At the village. He wants each team to remain spread out, so if there's a building in your path, don't go round it, go through it.
Mouth What's he on about?
Sir You're doing it again. Shut up. Is it totally beyond your control to remain silent just for a minute? We miss so much. You cause so much trouble. We'd be better off a dumb mute.
Ears You listening?
Sir I'm listening, carry on.
Ears If a building lies in your path, don't——
Sir (*to Mouth*) You just don't seem to know when to keep quiet. That's the problem.

There is a pause

Ears If a building lies in your path——
Sir Is it something I've done? Have I hurt you in some way?
Ears Have you done?
Sir Yes I've done.
Ears You sure?
Sir I'm sure.

There is a pause

Ears If a building——
Sir Please. Just try to keep quiet.

There is a pause

Ears If a building lies in your path, don't go round it. Go through it. Go through the window ...
Eyes Platoon's falling out.
Sir What, briefing's finished?
Eyes That's right.
Sir But we haven't heard all that's been said yet.
Ears I'm about to tell you what was said.

Our Man

Eyes They're moving out to board the trucks.
Sir We'd better follow.
Ears What about the briefing?
Sir You can tell me as we go along. General command, Phones. Follow out platoon.
Ears I'm not telling you what was said until you're listening.
Sir I'm listening now.
Phones "Follow platoon out. Usual routine."
Ears He said that he ... I can't remember where I was now.
Sir If a building lies in our path. Something like that.
Ears You remembered.
Sir Of course I did. Do you think I haven't been listening?
Phones Have we picked up Our Man's gear yet, Eyes?
Eyes Yeah. Gun, ammo. We've got the lot.
Sir All right. Um. Go on from there, Ears.
Ears Right. Um. Yeah. If a building lies in your path, don't go round it, go through it ... right?
Sir Right.
Ears Go through the window——
Eyes Hey, it's been snowing.
Sir You're joking?
Eyes No. See for yourself.
Sir (*looking at the screen*) I hope it doesn't hinder operations.
Eyes No, it won't It's not very thick.
Ears I haven't told you all the briefing yet.
Sir No. No. Carry on then, Ears.
Ears If a building lies in ... No, we've done that. He wants us to go through the window ...
Sir Phones. You'd better tell the Feet to tread carefully in case of ice.
Nose I love that clean fresh smell.
Ears Go through a window, door, up the drainpipe——
Sir How many trucks are there?
Eyes Three.
Sir There should be six. So three have gone already.
Eyes We want to board the one on the left.
Sir Do that, Phones. Carry on, Ears.
Phones Board truck on the left. General command.
Ears Up the drainpipes and through the skylight ...
Sir What are you talking about?

Ears This is what Barker wants us to do.
Sir Oh.
Ears You know. Instead of going round a building.
Sir Oh yes. That's right.
Phones How we doing, Eyes?
Eyes Left more.
Phones Left more.
Sir What did he say then?
Ears You sure you want to know?
Sir Of course I do. What did he say?
Ears You haven't exactly been listening to me so far.
Sir Just tell me what he said.
Eyes Left more.
Phones More to the left.
Ears All right. He wants us to go through anything. Anything as long as we stay spread out.
Eyes Left more.
Phones More to the left.
Ears It's like a soccer match, he said. He wants to stretch their defences.
Eyes More to the left, Phones.
Phones You sure?
Eyes To the left more.
Ears He wants to stretch their defences——
Phones More to the left.
Ears By keeping our attack wide.
Sir Quite an effective little allegory.
Ears Allergy what?
Sir Did he say anything else?
Eyes Left more.
Ears Yeah. He wants to stop them forming a nucleus around the goal.
Phones More to the left.
Sir Same thing really to what he said before.
Ears That's Barker though, isn't it. He always says more than he should.
Eyes Left more, Phones.
Phones Are you sure?
Eyes Yes. To the left more.
Sir How's it going, Phones?

Our Man

Phones We're taking an awfully long time getting to this truck.
Sir Where's the truck now, Eyes?
Eyes Truck?
Sir The one we're supposed to be boarding.
Eyes Truck. Oh. That truck! I don't know.
Sir What do you mean?
Eyes I don't know.
Sir What do you mean you don't know?
Eyes I was watching the Feet make footprints in the snow.
Sir Making footprints in the snow?
Eyes No-one saw us. Except Parsons.
Sir Parsons saw?
Eyes He was doing it too.
Sir Get us to that truck. Get us there right now. This second.
Eyes It's ... it's over there. (*He points*)
Phones Where's over there?
Eyes To the right more.
Phones Board truck on right. General command.
Sir Board truck to right quickly, Phones.
Phones Board truck quickly, i.e. run.
Eyes We're running.
Sir I don't know what you're doing, Eyes.
Eyes It's fun seeing Feet fit into footprints Feet have made before first time round. Ah. We're in the truck.
Phones Can we sit?
Eyes Yeah.
Phones Where can we sit?
Eyes We can sit where we're standing now.
Phones Sit.
Eyes We're sat.
Sir Where are we sat?
Eyes At the end of the bench on the right wall of the truck by the tailgate. Parson's opposite us and Hesketh's on our right.
Mouth Where's Flemings?
Eyes Search me.
Sir Is he in the truck?
Eyes Don't think so. Turn the Head round to the right, Phones.
Phones Neck turn Head out to the right.
Eyes No. He's not here.
Phones Thank you. He must have gone ahead in another truck.

Eyes What's that? (*He points*)
Sir I don't know. You're the Eyes.
Eyes (*turning his hand*) A dead one of those.
Sir No, I'm sorry. That's enough. We're here to fight a battle. We can't behave like school children. From now on I want maximum efficiency. Let's get ready for combat action. All right?
All Sir.
Ears Ignition key's turning. Engine is revving and we're off.
Eyes We're moving away from the church.
Sir What can you see ahead of us?
Eyes I don't know. I can't see ahead because it's a covered truck. I can only see behind. Over the tailgate. Flat fields stretching to distant hills. A few trees. Leafless. Rows of walls and hedges. Everything covered in a white coating of snow. Sky is blue. The odd cloud. Very little wind.
Ears I can't hear anything because of the engine.
Mouth Shall I start to sing a song?
Sir I don't think that's very sociable.
Mouth I'll do it quietly.
Sir Leave it, Mouth. Phones?
Phones Sir?
Sir Have a word with CNS. Remind them today is just a mopping-up operation. Nothing like yesterday.
Phones I'm sure they'll be pleased to hear that.
Sir Good.
Mouth Why not, "It's a long way to Tipperary"?
Sir No, Mouth. I told you once and I won't tell you again. No singing.
Ears My ears are cold. Phones, have the Hands rub the Ears will you.
Phones Hello, Central Nervous System. Phones of the Head Department. Be with you in a minute, Ears.
Nose That's funny.
Sir What?
Nose I could have sworn I smelt a cruise in the Mediterranean in warm sun, sipping Martinis with an orchestra playing in the background.
Eyes That was Our Man's honeymoon.
Phones But there's no need to worry.
Nose Must have been the truck's diesel fumes. Reminds me of the liner's engine room.

Our Man

Phones Today's not going to be anything like yesterday. It's just a mopping-up operation ... Oh, well, please yourself.
Sir Problems.
Phones I told CNS not to worry about today, but they're still worried.
Sir They're an odd bunch. What would ever happen if CNS got control of the Head Department?
Mouth Insanity.
Eyes Nothing's happening outside. We're moving quite fast.
Sir How fast?
Eyes At about ... about ... fifty ... fifty miles an hour.
Sir How long before we reach the crossroads at that speed? Our debarkation point?
Phones Not more than five minutes I'm sure.
Sir We'll be in the thick of the battle by then.
Nose So, five minutes in which to prepare ourselves?
Eyes The rest are getting ready.
Sir Such as?
Eyes Parson's picking his nose.
Ears Is that all?
Eyes He's eating it too.
Ears Yeah, but it's a strange way to calm the system.
Eyes Haines is kissing a rabbit's foot.
Mouth He's always kissing that rabbit's foot. If he's not kissing a rabbit's foot, he's kissing Barker's Foot. The creep.
Eyes Vickers is chewing gum. As cool as ever.
Phones He's psycho that's why.
Ears Hesketh's saying a prayer.
Sir Fair enough.
Eyes Wilkins is twitching like a decapitated chicken.
Phones He'll be the first to go. CNS have a strong hold on his Head Department.
Nose What do we do before combat?
Mouth We get sick. That's a point. (*He looks down the mouth tube*)
Sir Anything there?
Mouth No. Nothing.
Phones That's unusual.
Mouth Wait a minute. I see it. It's on the way up.
Sir Why do they always do this?
Phones Central Nervous System, why did you issue Stomach with a regurgitation command? (*After a pause to Sir*) Because they're

worried. They have the impression that we are not worried, that we think it's just going to be like a stroll in the park, so they're worried.

Mouth Well, tell them I'm worried to. It's at Larynx level!

Phones What if we ask Stomach to take it back?

Sir It's worth a try. Get on to CNS again first.

Mouth Must you?

Phones Central Nervous System, we appreciate your concern and will endeavour to take more care.

Mouth It's got to a couple of Taste Buds.

Phones Stomach. Urgent favour please. Could you take back the regurgitation you sent up? No. Not for good. Just till a more opportune moment should arise.

There is a pause

Sir What do they say?

Phones Unsympathetic. We sent the rubbish down, now we can have it back.

Mouth It's got to go!

Eyes Neck stretch Head out over the tailgate, Phones.

Phones Neck stretch Head out over tailgate.

Mouth The Taste Buds can't stand it any longer!

Eyes No! Neck's going the wrong way! We're pointing at Hesketh. He's on our right. We want to go to the left.

Phones Wrong way, Neck. To the left. Go to the left.

Eyes Now we're looking straight ahead. We're pointing straight at Parsons! You should see his face!

Phones Turn, Neck. Turn.

Eyes Again! Wrong way! To the left!

Phones Left, Neck! Left!

Eyes It's there!

Mouth It's going.

Eyes I can see it going.

Sir Is it still going?

Eyes Still going.

Sir Has it gone?

Eyes Still going ... going ... gone.

Mouth It's gone.

Sir Thank goodness for that.

Eyes You should have seen Parson's face when he thought he was going to get it. Never in the field of human conflict ...

Mouth What a load of sods Stomach are. They could have taken that back quite easily.
Ears In a way it's only fair. We have somewhat abused Stomach.
Mouth Smother them in castor oil and antibiotics. That's what I say.
Ears Just think, if we're going home soon, we won't have to put up with beans and canteen coffee any more. We can go back to real home cooking.
Nose I wish we could do that cruise again. The one I smelt earlier.
Eyes I'd rather a cup of tea in front of the fire.
Ears Rhubarb crumble.
Sir She does a lovely rhubarb crumble.
Mouth Or apple pie.
Ears Yes. That and cold vanilla ice cream melting on the top.
Mouth Did you hear that, Buds? Eh? Hot apple pie with cold ice cream melting on the top? Ha, ha, ha.
Sir Don't tease them, Mouth.
Eyes Truck's stopped.
Phones Lemon meringue pie.
Sir What about the main course?
Nose Roast beef. Yorkshire pud and potatoes. A real Sunday roast. Smelling it on the way back from the pub.

They all lurch

Sir What was that?
Eyes Hesketh's just pushed us.
Sir Tell him to sod off.
Mouth With the greatest of pleasure.
Eyes Wait. He's pushed us because we've arrived.
Sir Arrived?
Eyes We're there. It's jump-out time and into battle.
Sir Oh, God. Right, come one. Let's get things moving. Out truck, Phones.
Phones Jump out of truck.
Sir Adrenalin drive.
Phones This is Adrenalin drive. Adrenalin drive.
Sir Let's cross fingers.
Phones Cross fingers.
Eyes Teams fanning out.
Ears Gunfire from all directions.
Sir Keep the Head down.

Eyes Flemings' truck's got here before us.
Ears We've got to move.
Sir What's the best way for us to go?
Eyes We want to go over a wall to our right and cross a pasture.
Phones Jump wall.
Sir Where are we in relation to the village?
Eyes It's some way off to our left.
Phones Cross pasture.
Ears Shots coming from our right!
Eyes There's some buildings there. They've been shelled good and proper.
Sir Are there men in there?
Eyes I think so.
Sir They'll be ours. Let's go over there and help them. Fast as possible, but keep Our Man down. Phones?
Phones Everything's working fine, Sir.
Eyes I can see some enemy, Sir.
Sir Where?
Eyes Far away on our left. They haven't seen *us* yet.
Sir Let's make sure they don't.
Eyes There's an old dilapidated barn a hundred yards away!
Sir Head for it. Maybe we can pick them off from there. Move. Move.
Phones Run.
Eyes There's a wall ahead!
Sir Jump it.
Phones Jump wall.
Eyes Now a field. A ploughed field.
Sir Run it.
Phones Run.
Eyes There's a wall on our left obscuring our view of the enemy.
Sir Good, that means they can't see *us*.
Eyes We're coming to a break in the wall!
Sir Hit the ground!
Phones Hit ground.
Sir Shuffle.
Phones Shuffle.
Sir Can they still see us?
Eyes (*after a slight pause*) No. We've cleared the break.
Sir Right. Run, Phones.

Phones We're running.
Nose I can smell cow dung.
Ears Shooting from inside the barn!
Sir They're our boys.
Eyes Wall ahead, then about five yards to the barn.
Sir Jump it and get inside the barn.
Phones We've jumped it.
Eyes There's a door!
Sir Get in. Out of view. (*He looks out of eyes' screen*)
Eyes You'll have to open it.
Sir Kick it.
Phones Kick down door.
Eyes We're in. Two men! Soldiers! They're not ours! They're them!
Sir (*running to Phones; yelling into the microphone*) Shoot! Shoot!

We hear the sound of gunfire

Eyes Two of them taken by surprise ...
Sir Not half as much as we.
Eyes Both raising their guns. The first, from the left, not a chance.
Sir Thank God we are quick.
Eyes Our machine gun's entered him, spraying across the chest. Lots of blood spurting out. The second's had more time to pull the trigger. We may have been hit! (*He turns to Phones*)
Sir Phones?
Phones No data yet.
Nose I can smell farmhouse straw.
Eyes Wait! Wait! Yes, our bullets have entered him!
Sir I hope to God there's no-one else in the barn out of sight.
Eyes They've gone in the top half of the chest. A little higher and you'll get him in the throat and head. It's there! He's a gonner! Blood all over the place.
Sir Anyone else in the barn?
Eyes I don't think so. I think we're safe.
Sir Are we hit?
Phones Negative. All in order.
Eyes Wait. There is someone else! In the corner! Crouching!
Sir Shoot him!
Eyes He's one of ours!
Sir Cancel!

Phones Cancelled.

There is a pause

Sir How is he?
Ears He's groaning.
Eyes He's in a pretty bad way.
Sir Who is it?
Eyes It's hard to tell.
Sir Can we help him? (*He looks out of Eyes' screen*)
Eyes Have a look and see for yourself.
Sir Mmm. Maybe if we can get him back to base——
Eyes Maybe.
Sir Just a minute ... it's Flemings, isn't it?
Eyes I think you're right. It is! It's Flemings!

There are various exclamations as they all go to look out of Eyes' screen

Nose How did he get here?
Mouth That's him out of the promotion stakes.
Ears How can you say that?
Mouth Just a thought.
Eyes He's pretty far gone.
Nose Look at his face.
Phones Unless he dies fast, he'll be swamped with pain signals.
Ears Poor bastard.
Eyes (*noticing in the corner of the screen*) Aagh! One of them's still alive! He's raising his gun! He's going to try to shoot us!

They all try to rush back to their posts. It is chaos

Eyes He's pulled the trigger!
Phones (*finally arriving at the microphone*) Shoot! Shoot!
Eyes Bullets are coming at us!

We hear the rattle of gunfire

Phones We've been hit!

There is a short Black-out and silence. Then the Lights and sound return

   We still have hold of the gun!
Sir Keep hold of it!

Mouth Has he killed us?
Sir Eyes! Get back to your post!
Mouth Has he?
Sir Get back to your post. Eyes! What do you see?
Mouth Has he killed us?
Sir Shut up!

When Eyes reaches his post there is a full burst of light and the gunfire stops

Eyes The enemy's collapsed, but when he recovers he'll try for us again.
Phones We still have hold of the gun.
Ears Shoot him!
Sir Shoot!
Phones Shoot!

There is a pause

Nose Nothing's happening.
Phones The Arm won't respond!
Mouth He's killed us! He's bloody well killed us!
Eyes It's the Shoulder! The Shoulder's been hit!
Sir (*rushing to look out of Eyes' screen*) Which Shoulder?
Eyes Right Shoulder.
Phones Right Shoulder's preventing right Arm from raising the gun!

Sir rushes out

Ears Where's he going?
Eyes He's going to try and move right Arm himself.
Ears He'll never do it in time.
Eyes What else do you suggest?
Nose Something doesn't smell too good.
Mouth What are you on about?
Nose I don't know, but something's wrong.
Ears I can hear a noise ... the enemy's stirring!
Eyes Yeah ... Yes, he's gaining consciousness!
Mouth Phones?
Eyes He's seen us!
Mouth What's happening, Phones?
Eyes He's raising his gun!

Phones He's there! Sir's there!
Eyes Yes. Yes. I can see the Arm moving!
Phones Come on, Sir: shoot!
Eyes We're not going to make it!
Nose What's this smell?

Gunfire rattles

Eyes Bullets. Bullets flying backwards and forwards ... He's hit! He's been hit! Oh my God, we've done it!

There are various whoops for joy and "Well done, Sir's"

Nose (*in the midst of the celebrations*) No. Wait! Listen! Listen a minute! What's this smell? What is it?
Mouth What's the matter?
Nose I can smell something and I don't know what it is!
Mouth Who cares.
Nose No. No. It's like damp cardboard boxes!
Ears What are you talking about?
Nose Listen. Listen. Phones. Our Man was pushing Harry along the canal one day. This summer. Helen was with us too. Harry was still in the pram. It was Our Man's wedding anniversary.
Mouth When we were talking about what we wanted Harry to be when he grows up?
Nose That's right. There was lots of scents. Lime trees. The beer garden. Canal water. But there was another scent I can't recall. Something happened.

There is a pause

Eyes We were walking under a bridge.
Nose That's right, we were walking under a bridge.
Ears I could hear the pram wheels rolling over shale, slightly echoey under the bridge.
Eyes We were looking forwards, beyond the bridge. The tow-path led round, up and over us. Immediately in front was a green weeping willow. Outbuildings behind. On the other side of the canal, where we were going to cross to, was a green park lined with dark green lime trees and black railing. The sky was light blue. Early evening. Ducks on the water. Swallows darting over, catching flies.
Nose It was a bird. Another sort of bird.

Eyes At the corner of the tow-path as it left to cross the bridge, lay a swan.
Nose That's it!
Mouth It was a young swan.
Nose Which a dog had got at.
Eyes And ripped its belly wide apart.
Mouth Its intestines were hanging out.
Nose That's the smell. That's the sort of subtle, delicate scent I associate with giblets and things.
Phones So what's the point of all this?
Nose That's what I can smell now.

There is a pause

Phones (*listening on the earphones*) I'm not getting any signals.
Eyes Take a look at this.

Phones goes to Eyes' screen and looks

Ears What is it, Phones?

Phones goes back to his desk

Eyes We've been ripped apart. Our Stomach's hanging out.

There is a pause as they look at Phones

Nose Phones?

There is a pause

Ears What about the Heart, Phones?
Phones (*taking off the earphones*) It's not responding.

They all leave their posts, shutting down as they do. Eyes closes the shutters. Someone switches on the light. They all stand around Phones

Ears Are you sure?
Phones I can't get a signal.

There is a pause

Nose The Heart's stopped?
Mouth If it's not responding then the Heart's stopped.
Phones I think it's stopped.

Sir enters

Sir Right. Come on. Let's get Our Man moving. We've spent too much time in this barn.
Ears The Heart's stopped, Sir.

There is a pause

Sir Rubbish. It can't have.
Phones I'm afraid it has, Sir.
Sir What do you see, Eyes?
Eyes I can't see anything. Nothing's functioning any more.
Sir Come on. What do you see?
Eyes Nothing.
Sir Think.

There is a pause

Eyes I can't see anything.
Sir Where are we?
Eyes I don't know.
Sir Come on. Where are we? Think.
Eyes Well, in the barn, I suppose.
Sir Exactly. In the barn. And where's the door?
Eyes The door?
Sir It's behind us, isn't it?
Eyes Oh ...
Sir Where's the door?
Eyes Behind us.
Sir Is it open or shut?
Eyes Shut. No. It's open.
Sir Good. So now we know where we are. Don't we?
Eyes Yes.
Sir So we know where we have to go to get out, don't we? Ears, what can you hear?
Ears Nothing.
Sir Come on. There's guns firing in the distance, aren't there?
Ears Yes ...
Sir What else can you hear?
Ears I don't know.
Sir The wind. Rustle of leaves ...
Ears Yes ...
Sir What else? What else can you hear?
Ears A chicken. A chicken outside.

Sir What do you smell, Nose?
Nose Er? Er ...
Sir Blood. Lots of it. What does blood smell like?
Nose Damp cardboard boxes.
Sir Try again.
Nose A butcher's shop!
Sir (*after a pause*) That'll do. So. Eyes can see. What do you see, Eyes?
Eyes Lots of blood. Dead enemy. Barn. Door behind which is open.
Sir Ears can hear. What do you hear, Ears?
Ears Distant guns. Leaves rustling. The wind. A duck. I mean a chicken.
Sir What do you smell, Nose?
Nose A butcher's shop.
Sir Phones. Give the order for Our Man to crawl for the door.
Phones But the Heart's not functioning, Sir ...
Sir It is functioning. We'll get Our Man moving even if I have to go through to each department and do it myself.
Mouth Tell him it's functioning, Phones.
Eyes No. Don't. This is ridiculous. The Heart isn't functioning. Nothing's functioning. I can't see. Ears, Ears, can't hear, can you, Ears?
Ears No. I can't hear anything.
Eyes Nose, doesn't smell anything ...
Nose I can't smell anything.
Eyes And Mouth. Mouth can't say anything.
Mouth It doesn't leave much to be said.
Eyes Exactly, we are dead. Our Man is dead.

There is a Black-out and a long silence

Ears What do you want to be next time round, Phones?
Phones I'm not too sure. Give me a hand with these, will you?
Ears Those our records?
Phones Enables Central Sorting Office to assess past performance when awarding future posting.
Eyes I'd like to be in a painter next time round.
Nose Who's that bunch over there?
Sir Is it Flemings' people?
Eyes Who was Flemings?

Sir He was ... He was Our Man's rival.
Eyes Rival in what?
Sir I can't remember.
Nose How far do we have to go?
Phones Till we get there I suppose.
Eyes It's a bit like walking in space, isn't it?
Mouth Did you say those were our records, Phones?
Phones Yes.
Mouth How did we do?
Phones I can't remember. It's all written down here.

There is a pause

Ears I can't remember anything about it now.
Nose Nor can I.
Phones (*after a pause*) Let's hope next time round's as much fun.
Mouth I wonder what we'll be in.
Nose You'll probably be in a garden slug.
Phones Half way up Nelson's column in a coconut.
Mouth What are you talking about?
Phones I don't know. I must be dreaming.

CURTAIN

FURNITURE AND PROPERTY LIST

On stage: TV
Food tube
Screen with shutters
Desk. *On it:* microphone, files, progress report
Chair

Personal: **Phones:** earphones

LIGHTING PLOT

Practical fitting required: TV screen

To open: dark stage except for blue light from TV

Cue 1	**Eyes** opens the shutters *Light seeps in*	(Page 2)
Cue 2	**Phones:** "We've been hit!" *Black-out, pause, then bring up lighting as before*	(Page 28)
Cue 3	When **Eyes** reaches his post *Full burst of light*	(Page 29)
Cue 4	**Eyes** closes the shutters *Dim lighting*	(Page 31)
Cue 5	Someone switches on the light *Snap on light*	(Page 31)
Cue 6	**Eyes:** "Our Man is dead." *Black-out*	(Page 33)

EFFECTS PLOT

Cue 1	**Sir:** "Shoot! Shoot!" *Sound of gunfire*	(Page 27)
Cue 2	**Eyes:** "... coming at us!" *Rattle of gunfire*	(Page 28)
Cue 3	**Phones:** "We've been hit!" *Short silence then gunfire*	(Page 28)
Cue 4	When **Eyes** reaches his post *Gunfire stops*	(Page 29)
Cue 5	**Nose:** "What's this smell?" *Rattle of gunfire*	(Page 30)

MADE AND PRINTED IN GREAT BRITAIN BY
LATIMER TREND & COMPANY LTD PLYMOUTH
MADE IN ENGLAND

www.ingramcontent.com/pod-product-compliance
Ingram Content Group UK Ltd.
Pitfield, Milton Keynes, MK11 3LW, UK
UKHW021840210426